MW01048407

saying yes to being a Christian

Herbert O'Driscoll

Anglican Book Centre
Toronto, Canada

1995
Anglican Book Centre
600 Jarvis Street
Toronto, Ontario
M4Y 2J6

Canadian Cataloguing in Publication Data

O'Driscoll, Herbert, 1928–
    Baptism : saying yes to being a Christian

(Pastoral series)
ISBN 1-55126-131-6

1. Baptism.   I. Title.   II. Series: O'Driscoll, Herbert,
1928–   .   Pastoral series

BV811.2.037 1995   234'.161   C95-932344-9

Give them a spirit
to know and love you,
and the gift of joy and wonder
in all your works.

Book of Alternative Services, page 160

Herbert O'Driscoll has written many popular books on Bible interpretation and Celtic spirituality. A well-known broadcaster and speaker, he has travelled widely throughout North America, Europe, and the Holy Land. In this series he explains, clearly and simply, what it means to be a Christian, and shows how Christianity enriches our everyday living.

Books in this series include

About This Book

If you are about to become a Godparent, or if you yourself are thinking about Christian baptism, or if you have been asked to act as sponsor for an adult friend or relative in his or her baptism, this book will be of interest to you.

Baptism is central in Christian faith. Jesus, who gave very few commands, gave us the command to baptize. In the early days of Christian faith, to be baptized was costly and even dangerous. Today, this remains true in many parts of the world. To be baptized as an adult means that we commit ourselves to Christian faith, to involvement in the life of the Christian community, and to living as a Christian in the world. We believe that we are given grace to help us in these intentions.

To be baptized as a child is likewise to receive the grace of our Lord Jesus Christ to live as a faithful Christian, but years of faithful guiding and nurturing are called for in this formation. That is why the invitation to be a Godparent should never be given or accepted lightly.

Long ago, Christian life developed a tradition called *Anam-cara*. In Gaelic, the word *anam* means 'soul,' and the word *cara* means 'friend.' Early Christians considered it very important to have a soul friend on the journey through life. That is what we become when we stand beside a friend or relative at their baptism, or when we stand as Godparent at a child's baptism. We promise to become that person's soul friend. When or if we offer ourselves for baptism in our adult years, we too need someone to be *Anam-cara* to us, a Christian friend to accompany us on our eternal journey through life and beyond.

Herbert O'Driscoll

The short title at the top of each of these pieces is taken from the church's service of Baptism. When you have read this little book you may wish to look at that service. If so, you can find it on page 151 of one of the church's prayer books called *The Book of Alternative Services*. There is also a service of Baptism on page 532 in *The Book of Common Prayer*. Copies of both of these books can be found in most Anglican churches.

The grace of our Lord Jesus Christ, and the love of God, and the fellowship of the Holy Spirit be with you all.

When people meet, they almost always greet one another. Even in our hurried and crowded lives, we instinctively want to offer some sort of greeting, no matter how casual. We meet in an elevator, a crowded bus, a movie line-up, a crosswalk, and our instinct is to say at least a brief Hi or Hello.

The truth is that we are not meant to be alone. This is stated in the first pages of the Bible, and this is what we acknowledge as the first thing when we take part in Christian baptism. We talk about three things we all need and wish for one another.

The first is *grace*. None of us can live entirely from our own resources. We need encouragement, guidance, direction, discipline, friendship, affection, and love from others. Christians take this thought one step further. Christians believe that all these things that we get through other people come from Jesus Christ. He is the ultimate source of grace.

The second thing we all need is *love*, so that we may ourselves give it to others. The second part of this statement is important, because we live in a culture that is very 'me' directed. I need love. I want love. But a Christian writer named C. S. Lewis once pointed out that what he called 'need love' is not enough. We also have to have what he called 'give love.' That's the love we offer others. Once again Christian faith adds something to this. A Christian believes that the ultimate source of love is above and beyond us, in God.

We wish each other *fellowship*. We need one another. Notice how we trace this fellowship back to God's Holy Spirit. We're saying that if Christians share a belief in God, and if they believe that God reached out and touched our humanity in Jesus Christ, then we share a Spirit, a way of thinking about life, and a way of living it. This Spirit gives life a kind of wholeness. That's why we call it the Holy Spirit.

We have only just begun, and we've already said a lot about the Christian faith.

Alleluia! Christ is risen.
The Lord is risen indeed. Alleluia!

We don't just say this. We almost shout it! You may not hear this at every baptism, because it is used as a greeting only at certain times of the year. It might be wise to use it all the time, though, because it is the single most important part of Christian faith. That's the reason why we don't just mumble it. We shout it, or if we don't, we should!

Why should we shout out this greeting? Because if Jesus Christ had not risen from the dead, you would not be reading these pages, and you wouldn't be involved in someone else's baptism or considering it for yourself. If Jesus had not risen, there would not have been an original Christian community. Jesus would have been remembered for a while, just as we remember any great man or woman. But two thousand years after he walked among us as a human being, Jesus is utterly real to millions of people, so real that even in the twentieth century some are quite ready to die—and have done so—for the belief they have in him.

Notice the small but hugely significant word *is* in the statement, 'Christ *is* risen.' We don't just say that Christ rose. We say that he *is risen*. There is a huge difference. The first statement describes a long-ago historical event. The second is an on-going reality, real in the present and continuing to be real in the future. A Christian believes that Jesus is alive.

How do Christians explain this? How do they prove it? They don't do either. They come at it in a very different way. They test it out. They decide that they will begin to live as if it were true that Jesus is risen. They then find out in their experience that it is true. And so we have millions of Christian lives of every conceivable kind—rich and poor, wise and simple, young and old—lived out in generation after generation.

Think of this when you see some of them at this coming baptism.

There is one body and one Spirit,
There is one hope in God's call to us;
One Lord, one faith, one baptism,
One God and Father of all.

Like a lot of things in Christian worship, this is a kind of song, and like all good songs, it has a beat and a good climax. The beat in the song comes in the word *one*. We say it again and again, seven times in four lines, so it is not difficult to pick out the important idea the church is trying to tell us here. It's all in that word *one*.

In another place and time, God gave us an all-important message centred around the word *one*. Thousands of years ago, when the people of Israel were at Mount Sinai during their long, tough journey to their own land, they learned that whatever else God is, God is one God. That is a huge statement with many layers of meaning, but the bottom line is that all reality, all creation, is linked together, interrelated like a vast web. It is fascinating how God is teaching us this again today through the sciences, especially the micro-sciences.

At the same time, we are being told something else. Not only is all created reality one, but this one vast web is sacred. It does not just exist. It is holy! At the moment of baptism we are saying this again, in a different way. The whole creation is both a living body and a spirit. Some modern Christian thinkers tell us that we need to begin to think of the planet itself, even of the galaxies, as nothing less than part of the body of God. To think like this about creation is wonderfully hopeful, and this is 'one hope' we can all share.

The song then shifts to Jesus, and it assures us about something that very often troubles people. For there is no end to the ways in which Jesus is spoken about and presented, no end to the many varieties of Christian faith, and no end to the forms of Christian community that invite us to join them. We do not discuss this in the baptismal service. Instead we make the simple statement that, above and beyond all these variations and forms, there is the sublime reality of Jesus Christ, who offers us faith and calls us to respond.

I present N. to receive the sacrament of baptism. (said by a sponsor)

At this moment a lovely event takes place. Notice that it doesn't matter whether the person being presented for baptism is an adult or a child. In each case someone else presents him or her for baptism. This person could be a parent or some other relative, a Godparent, a friend, a spouse. The point is that the person to be baptized is very dear to the presenter. Someone for whom Christian faith is already a reality is saying to the church, 'Here is someone I value and love, and for whom I wish the precious thing I myself have found— faith in Jesus Christ.' What could be more natural than wishing that another may have what we ourselves have found invaluable?

However, if you do this, especially if you do it for a child, then you accept the accompanying responsibility. What happens on this particular day is only the first sentence in a story that never ends. So it follows that you can't just step into this person's life, bring them to baptism, make some promises, and then step back and walk away. If you are presenting an adult friend, then this baptism binds you even closer in friendship, for now you both have another friend in common—Jesus Christ.

If you are presenting a child for baptism, then what happens at that baptism bestows the immense privilege of sharing in the formation of a human life and of the spirit within that life. You have accepted the responsibility of making sure that this child becomes aware of Jesus Christ as someone uniquely significant for him or her.

But you will also promise to stay in for the long haul. Before this child lies the journey to maturity. To become mature means to become the best we can be, to become as completely fit for life as possible. For a Christian, the ultimate model of the best is seen in Jesus. This is what you want for this child who means so much to you as parent or Godparent. This is why you will say, 'I will,' when you are asked for these promises. Even as you answer, you will be only too aware of your own limitations. Knowing this, you will ask for God's help in the task ahead.

Do you renounce Satan and all the spiritual forces of wickedness that rebel against God?

Suddenly we are using very tough and rather ominous words! We knew that baptism was serious, but does it have to get *this* serious?

Yes, it does, because evil is a reality. This is not to say that Christians believe that people are evil, period. Christians are not saying that creation is evil, or that all the structures and institutions we live in are evil. After all, on the very first page of the Bible it is stated that God looked at all creation and saw that it was good.

But the Bible also points out—and Christians believe—that evil entered into this creation and into human nature itself, and therefore into everything that we humans form and build. Nowadays we use other words for evil. We say that things have a dark side—remember Darth Vader in Star Wars?—or we say with Carl Jung that human nature has a shadow side.

Within Christian faith, this kind of language is not strong enough to name something that needs to be faced realistically. Christian faith maintains that evil is not just the dark side of good, or the shadow side of light. This is to see evil as not real in itself but as merely an aspect of good, even the absence of good. Christians believe that evil is a reality in itself, and that it will remain in human nature and in human affairs until the end of time. If we doubt this, we have only to look in the mirror and face ourselves honestly. We have only to think of the elements of good and evil throughout all our institutions, including the places we work. When we do so, the phrase 'evil powers which corrupt and destroy' may not seem such an exaggeration.

When we speak of 'Satan and all the spiritual forces of wickedness rebelling against God,' we are trying to find words for an even greater and more mysterious possibility—that the struggle we know so well in our own lives and in human affairs is really just a local skirmish in a vast struggle that goes on at the heart of creation itself.

And we thought we were just baptizing someone! Is this a lot bigger than you thought? Yes it is. Let's keep going...

Do you renounce all sinful desires that draw you from the love of God?

At this point in the service, as we use phrases like 'spiritual forces,' 'evil powers,' and now 'sinful desires,' we seem to be dreaming up new book titles for either Susan Howatch or P. D. James. Both write English best-sellers and love book titles with religious undertones.

These phrases describe realities we all face in being human. Take this question about renouncing what we call 'sinful desires.' It is easy to read or hear these words and assume that Christian faith brands all human desires as sinful. Nothing could be further from the truth. After all, God gave us desires—artistic desires, material desires, sexual desires. The list is wonderful and endless. You and I just would not be human without desires. After all, none of us would exist had not those who gave us life desired each other!

Check out the words in the question that comes immediately before and after the word *desires*. We are not being asked to renounce our desires— to do so would mean ceasing to be human—but we are being asked to renounce *sinful* desires.

So which desires are sinful? Is there a neat and nasty list that Christian faith has all ready to hand us? The answer is a simple and very welcome one—No. Instead we are given a kind of measuring rod. A desire becomes sinful only on one condition—if it draws us from the love of God.

Isn't it fascinating how our supposedly turned on, freed up, laid back society almost always links the word *desire* with sex, as if there were no other desires? Desires are as varied as life itself. But they have one thing in common. They can become tyrants. They can take us over and make us slaves to them. That is what the baptism service is saying to us in this warning about being drawn from the love of God.

Makes a lot of sense when you think about it.

Do you turn to Jesus Christ and accept him as your Saviour?

We all know the moment when our dentist gives us an anesthetic before drilling. A good dentist has the needle in our gum before we know it. We rarely even see it in his or her hand.

It may seem strange to say so, but this moment in the baptismal service is not unlike that moment in our dentist's office. We are suddenly offered a gift, but since it comes with some cost, maybe even with some fear and pain, the gift is offered without warning.

Suddenly someone wants us to do something that will be costly. We are being asked to promise that we will respond to Jesus Christ in no less than four ways for the rest of our lives. To *turn* to him, *accept* him as Saviour, put our whole *trust* in him, and promise to *obey* him.

It's a tall order. It is so involved, we could write a book about it. But deep down, it is also very simple. We are being asked to choose a focus for our lives. Notice those four words—*turn, accept, trust, obey*. They are not separate realities. Given the first, the rest follow. If we really choose a course of action, a cause, a loyalty, a person, as ultimate for us, then we have in fact accepted it as something that makes all the difference for us. In that sense it saves us, and therefore, quite naturally, we trust in it and obey the demands it makes on us.

What we are being asked to do is to make the birth, life, suffering, death, and resurrection of Jesus the central focus of meaning in our lives. To do this requires some changes—some ways in which we *turn*—in our way of life. Then we have to *accept* the consequences. If we have chosen Jesus Christ as that which makes sense of life for us, then we *trust* that he will respond to our need for grace. And, since any relationship that is worthwhile demands that those in the relationship obey its demands, so we accept Jesus as our Lord and *obey* him.

Like all the really worthwhile and important things in life, maybe the only way to find out what it is like, is to try it.

Will you who witness these vows do all in your power to support these persons in their life in Christ?

Only a few weeks ago, I came very close to having to serve as a witness. As I approached a pedestrian crossing, a driver approaching it from the opposite direction glanced to the side for a moment. At that same moment, a child ran onto the crossing. The driver stopped just in time. If the worst had happened, I would have had to admit to being a witness.

Today, being a witness means something essentially passive. All I did was see something happen (in this case, the worst consequences were mercifully avoided). All I would have had to do as a witness was say that I had seen the event. Let's ignore my having to survive the onslaught of a defence lawyer.

To be a witness in terms of the Bible and Christian faith is something rather different. Much more is meant by the word witness. For a start, it means something active rather than passive. Here, we are being asked to do something as a consequence of witnessing this baptism. We are being asked to support this person for nothing less than the rest of his or her life. This support is of a particular kind. It means supporting this person 'in their life in Christ.'

These five words tell us a lot about the meaning of Christian faith. It is not merely knowing some facts about Jesus of Nazareth. It is about knowing him as a reality in our lives. These words are also saying to us that in Jesus Christ, not just in ourselves, we find what we need to be Christian. These simple but deep words are telling us that what happens at this baptism is only the beginning of something that will continue for a lifetime. If being Christian means that we have a relationship with Jesus Christ, then, as with any other relationship, it will either deepen or run the risk of fading away. The only certainty is that it will not stay the same.

Today we often use the phrase 'I'm not into that,' meaning that we are just not interested. Here at this baptism, we are using the words 'life *in* Christ' in a similar way. We are promising to do our best to help someone realize some day that they are really *into* Christ and Christian faith.

Let us now pray for these persons who are to receive the sacrament of new birth.

The pages of the Bible hum with constant activity. God is always coming and going, calling and creating, leading and guiding, warning and praising, and doing countless other things! The people in the Bible seem to be ceaselessly active—arguing and journeying and struggling and building and fishing, on and on, without ever stopping!

Notice the same kind of thing about the prayers that we are about to say for those to be baptized. We ask God to *deliver* them, *open* them, *fill* them, *teach* them, *send* them, *bring* them. If we add these verbs together, we come up with a God who is intensely involved and interested in human life.

In a mass culture and in an increasingly impersonal world, it may not be easy to believe that Christian faith offers us this truth about the nature of God as a grace and hope in our lives. We often hear people wonder aloud if their lives have any meaning. We hear of a friend who worked for a large corporation for years only to be thrown aside with a pink slip or, if he was fortunate, a severance package. In anger he will ask, 'What am I? Am I no more than a dispensable, throw-away object?'

Christian faith says a blunt and definite No to that. In this moment of baptism, a picture is drawn of a loving God intimately involved with the journey of human life, concerned and acting in this life even when the person makes no response and gives every indication that they couldn't care less.

At the end of these petitions, we say a prayer that expresses in its few short lines the heart of Christian faith. A Christian is a person who lives fully in the present, because he or she is linked both with the past and the future. A Christian looks back at the death of Jesus, lives day by day with the grace of Jesus, and looks ahead to a time when his or her own life, and all of creation, will reflect the glory of Jesus.

We give you thanks, almighty God and Father, for by the gift of water you nourish and sustain all living things.

We are nearing the moment of the actual baptism. The water is being poured into the font. As we do this, we tell some of the stories of the Christian community. Two of these stories are older than the Christian story. The first one is as old as creation itself.

As we tell this first story, we remind each other that all of creation begins with water. On the very first page of the Bible, we are shown the planet entirely covered with water. We see the Spirit of God hovering over this vast expanse. Then, echoing through the vastness of space, we hear the voice of that Spirit in majestic command—'Let the dry land appear.' We watch as the land rises from the waters over endless aeons to time. Then we see the land form into its ever-changing shapes, continents and islands, coastlines and estuaries, riverbeds and valleys, rockfaces and waterfalls. We realize that, without these waters endlessly rising and falling in their great tides, the land could not remain pure and fresh and fertile. We realize that, by the gift of water, God nourishes and sustains all living things.

We look into the water of the font, and we become aware of the world's need for clean water today, of the faces of those who must walk miles for it, of those who die for want of it. We are made to recall how the giving of even a fraction of our world's wealth to make water available would make so much difference.

We seem to have come a long way from the simplicity and intimacy of baptism, but we have not. All we have done is probe the deeper meaning of water as an element in God's creation. Water means life. Water means birth. This is what this occasion is about—new life and new birth for a new Christian. The same Holy Spirit that called the continents into being now calls someone we care for to become a new being, or calls us if we are the person to be baptized. That is the immensity and mystery of what is going on in this occasion.

And we thought we were just pouring water into a font!

We give you thanks that through the waters of the Red Sea, you led your people out of slavery to freedom in the promised land.

We are standing at the font. The water has been poured. That first story took us from the dawn of time to our own time of much privation and unequally distributed resources, especially clean water. Now we tell a second story, not as old, but still from a time long ago. It does not involve the whole span of creation, or even the whole of humanity. This is the story of a particular people.

We look into the font, and this time we see its absolute opposite, a bone-dry desert. In this desert we see a great gathering of people. When we look further, we see the terrible situation they are in. From behind, an army is about to attack them. In front, there is a wide expanse of water. As we watch, we see them move towards the wide mud flats, revealed by the retreating water. The fleeing people move across it successfully, but the heavily armoured chariots of their pursuers are engulfed in the mud and the returning water. The fugitives move on into the desert.

We are witnessing an event that the people of Israel saw ever afterwards as a death and resurrection experience. They risked death in the water, and they came through to find new life and a new future. In Egypt, they had been held as slaves. Moses led them to make their bid for freedom, and they succeeded. They entered the sea as slaves and emerged as free people.

What has this to do with bringing a person for baptism? The answer is in the water. Here it is being poured into the font. There, in that long ago story, the water is life-threatening, an expanse that cannot be safely crossed. The people could conceivably drown in it, but it turns out to be their path to survival and new life. To find that out, they must first risk dying.

The heart of this great insight into human experience is acted out in baptism. To obtain freedom and new life, we must risk the death of the old life. We learn this lesson again and again in life. It is taught here in the story we have just told, and even more explicitly in the story we are about to tell as we stand gathered around this water.

We give you thanks for sending us your son Jesus.

This is the story at the heart of Christian faith. Up to this point, Jesus has lived in Nazareth. Now he is some thirty years old, and he feels called to make a great change. He comes south to the river Jordan and is baptized. As this happens, he becomes deeply conscious that the Spirit of God is calling him

That is how baptism is understood—as a turning point. We see this quite clearly when we watch an adult being baptized. With a child, we see adults accepting the responsibility to help the child later to realize how and why his or her baptism can become the beginning of a turning towards Jesus as Lord.

Now we listen to something that sounds strange. We hear that 'Jesus suffered the baptism of his own death and resurrection, setting us free ... and opening to us ... everlasting life.' What has baptism to do with death and resurrection? They seem poles apart in human experience.

But this is not true. Look at what is done with the person to be baptized. He or she is put *under* the water. In most cases, this is done only symbolically. There are some new churches in various traditions that have returned to having a sunken area for baptisms, modelled on the fonts of earlier centuries. Some traditions of Christian faith never lost this tradition.

We are placed *under* the water. We are then led (a child is lifted) *from* the water. When this happens, a great truth is symbolized. We are told that in this moment something dies—our human nature as it is without God. And something comes into being—our human nature as it can be when permeated and transformed by God's Holy Spirit.

By going under this water we are saying (or having it said for us if a child), 'I want and need more than just my own human nature to live life as God calls and wills me to live it. I want a greater source of grace. I need a friend, an ally, a guide.' There is a word greater than any of these—we are expressing our need of a *Saviour*. That Saviour is Jesus.

We give you thanks for your Holy Spirit who teaches us and leads us into all truth, filling us with his gifts so that we might proclaim the gospel to all nations and serve you as a royal priesthood.

Have you noticed that all of these stories we tell while around the water begin with the words, 'We give you thanks'? Think of these stories for a moment as what we call 'sound bytes,' each of them emphasizing quickly and vividly an important aspect of Christian faith.

Have you noticed a tiny word, seemingly insignificant, that has begun to appear in these sound bytes? You could very easily miss it. It's the word *us*. We say that the Holy Spirit teaches and leads us 'so that we might proclaim ... and serve you.' A few moments ago, we said, 'For *us* Jesus was anointed, for *us* he suffered, setting *us* free.'

What is significant here is that you would expect everything about baptism to be personal and individual in focus and expression. In the sense that every life is uniquely significant, this is true. But Christian faith balances this. We are individuals, but we are also a people, a living body, a single entity at the centre of which Jesus stands and lives.

For instance, when we say that God's Holy Spirit fills us with gifts, we are not saying that each of us can have all of God's gifts. Each of us has gifts, but our gifts differ. It is only when we put our gifts together as a people of God that good and great things begin to happen. When we say that the Holy Spirit teaches us and leads us into all truth, this does not mean that each of us knows all truth. It is only as we share our insights about Jesus Christ, allowing these insights to refine and even correct one another, that we approach a vision of Jesus that reflects something of his reality.

Again, notice that we proclaim and serve Jesus. The way I try to proclaim him in my life may reach some people and alienate others. The way someone else proclaims him may succeed where I fail. The way I serve him will be incomplete. I have only so much time, so much energy, so much vision. But the service of others will compensate for my limitations.

Us and *we* are very big words in Christian faith, much bigger than *I*.

We give you thanks for you have called N.
to new life through the waters of baptism.

This is the moment when we ask God to put together all the stories we have just heard and to help them come true in the life of the person being baptized.

Once again, we say thank you. This time it's for a mysterious inner process that we can easily fail to recognize. Maybe we should ask a question or two. How and when were we called to sponsor this person for Christian baptism, to being a Godparent, or to be baptized ourselves? What is this inner voice that calls us in so many ways—many of them not recognizably religious? The answer is, God's Holy Spirit.

We are asking that the sequence of events in Jesus' life will now happen in the life of this person we care about, and in our own. He died and rose to new life. We all need to die to some of the old in our lives and start living to some of the new. We all want a sense that our life has been cleansed, that we can begin again without guilt or regrets. If a child is being baptized, all this is ahead for him or her.

We ask for the anointing of God's Holy Spirit. Think of the most wonderfully perfumed oil running over your body, giving you a sense of utter luxury and well-being. Does that sound like an advertisement for an expensive fragrance? If it does, all the copy writers in the commercial world couldn't find words to describe the anointing oils of God!

Why do we ask these things for the person being baptized? We want them to become what we call 'inheritors of your glorious kingdom.' We are asking of God that this person, who means so much to us, will discover that even to try to live according to the will of Jesus rather than by their own self-centred will can bring glimpses of glory and joy to their lives. When Jesus uses the term *kingdom*, he wants us to realize that if we genuinely try to live under the will of God, we catch glimpses in this life of a greater reality and a greater meaning. We glimpse a kingdom.

Do you believe in God the Father?

These days, Christians are once again trying to find words to describe God. God is beyond all language, so in different periods of history we have to search for new words, knowing they will fail in time. Even the word *God* is only a pathetic attempt to name the unimaginably profound source of all creation.

Nowadays, we tend to say that God is in creation. That is a great truth, and if we had held on to it in recent centuries, we might not be faced with the environmental problems we know so well. But it is not the whole truth. The whole truth is that God is in creation and at the same time above, beyond, and around it! What we are saying is that even if the whole universe ceased to be, God would not cease to be.

We are touching on what Christians believe about those vast cosmic issues that intrigue us all. Christian faith is not just about personal issues. It is not just about certain historical events, important as these are. Christian faith is not just some do's and don'ts for living. It is about all these things, but it extends into the furthest reaches of all we think about and imagine. Christian faith is a big faith.

Some people look at the words *creator of heaven and earth* and say, 'That was all very well as a concept when the human race pictured the universe as a rather small, up-down, three-tiered system.' But the words *heaven and earth* are infinitely adaptable. It matters not one bit that today we can look through the Hubble telescope and see a universe on a scale previous generations could not even imagine. The words 'heaven and earth' merely grow with these new realities and contain them easily!

The most important thing we are saying here is that we believe in God as *creator of heaven and earth*. This includes all of creation, including the Big Bang, the expanding universe, black holes, and anything else the mind of Stephen Hawking or anyone else can throw at us!

Do you believe in Jesus Christ, the Son of God?

Once again we try to find words to describe what no words will ever capture. Even Matthew, Mark, Luke, and John, who wrote the four Gospels for us, all wrestled for language to express what they believed about Jesus.

Notice the one thing that comes through in what we say about him. He was absolutely real. He lived at a certain time. He came up against powerful forces that eventually tortured and killed him. Then comes the heart of what Christians believe about him. He showed himself alive to those who had known him. He did this in such a real and vital way that those men and women who had been scattered and traumatized by his death re-gathered to become a movement that, within less than two hundred years, had spread throughout the very empire that had crucified him.

A Christian believes that when we look at Jesus Christ we are looking at a human being whose life was fully open to God, so open that Jesus' human will became fully one with God's will. The word that Christians use for this is *incarnation*. It's a Latin word that means 'God becomes flesh.'

Because this incarnation took place, Christians believe that something is now true for all human beings, something that is such good news that it takes a special word to express it—the word *gospel*. This gospel or good news is that, because Jesus opened himself fully to the presence of God, the divine presence has entered into human nature and human affairs. In a phrase, God is with us. There is even a single word that has passed into English that means this very thing. *Emmanuel* means 'God with us.'

This makes Jesus crucial to Christian faith. It makes him much more than merely the great teacher of the faith—Jesus is Christian faith! That is why Christians do not merely say, 'I believe Jesus Christ.' They say, 'I believe *in* Jesus Christ.' Many Christians do not fully realize this. It is a truth so enormous that it is difficult to grasp.

Come to think of it, if our minds could get around it without effort, it would not be such a great truth!

Do you believe in God the Holy Spirit?

The best way to understand what Christians mean when they say they believe in God's Holy Spirit is to look at what the Holy Spirit does. Interestingly, this is much the same as trying to understand wind. We cannot see wind, but the stronger it blows, the more easily we can see what it does. It is significant that the Hebrew word in the Bible for spirit, *ruach*, is also the name for the wind that blows from the desert.

The lines following this mention of the Holy Spirit tell us, in effect, what Christians believe the action of the Spirit of God to be. We see this if we read the rest of this statement of Christian faith as a sequence.

We can put it as follows: 'I believe in the Holy Spirit' who forms 'the holy catholic Church,' a fellowship that exists in the past, present, and future as 'the communion of saints,' in which we are accepted and loved by knowing that we receive 'the forgiveness of sins.' We also share a hope that our lives are destined for even greater meaning by 'the resurrection of the body,' whereby we experience 'everlasting life.'

No one would say that it is easy to believe all this. But then, anything that is easy to believe is probably not worth believing! It is possible to look at the statement above and see it as a magnificent description of the true context and meaning of human life. We certainly do not understand it, yet millions of men and women have lived their lives as if this faith were true. When they have done so, they have found that it is indeed true. The fact is, there is no other way to commit oneself to the Christian faith. Faith is not a matter of waiting until all guarantees are received, and all questions satisfactorily answered. If this were so, it would be something other than faith.

The words *Holy Spirit* are given another meaning at this point. Their first meaning is that of God's Holy Spirit, a spirit of love and creativity. To put it very simply, we believe that this is the Spirit that God brought to the forming of all creation. But we also believe that God has offered us this same Holy Spirit. It is within us as a kind of dim reflection, an echo of God that graces us and gives us the ability to love and to create.

Will you continue ... to persevere ... to proclaim ... to seek and serve Christ ... to strive for justice and peace...?

Notice that we now go further than a statement of belief, important as that is. We now face a number of questions that are not about believing but about doing. The Christian community is reminding us that this moment of baptism is only a beginning. We are being asked for an ongoing commitment, not merely to continue believing the Christian faith, but to go on living out the consequences of what we believe.

The first thing we might notice about the list of things we are asked to do is that none of them are what we would call neat, one-shot deals! All of them involve sticking with it, staying in for the long haul. The second thing they have in common is that they require an investment of ourselves. If we are being baptized as an adult, we are promising to do our best to meet these fairly challenging standards. If we are bringing a child for baptism, we are promising to try to form this child into the kind of person who will do these things.

Someone may ask, 'Do I have the right to ask

these things of a child? Surely a child has the right to decide for him or her self the kind of lifestyle they want.'

That statement reflects a belief that our culture has had us swallow—that all lifestyles are equally good. Only in recent years have people reawakened to the fact that believing this ensures a grim if not chaotic society. Is it really true that it doesn't matter what choices this child makes? It is interesting to see the return of a very old and half-forgotten idea—that true freedom is not the freedom to do what we like but the freedom to do what we ought!

Think about it. If you are a Christian parent or Godparent, all of these things you are asked to do are reasonable and integral elements in Christian faith. If you hesitate to make these promises, either as an adult coming for baptism or on behalf of a child being brought for baptism, maybe you need to ask yourself whether you wish to become—or to make this child—part of the Christian community.

Will you persevere?

We are still looking at those promises. Promises are never casual. Small children teach us this again and again. If we do not fulfil a promise made to a small child, he or she can be bitterly disappointed.

The promises we make at this baptism are not casual. In saying that we will 'continue in the apostles' teaching and fellowship,' we are promising to become aware of at least the main themes of the Christian faith and to participate in the sacred meal of the Christian community.

We promise to 'persevere in resisting evil.' We tend to think that there are certain major deeds that are evil. The melodramatic world of television encourages this. But for most of us, evil comes in ordinary ways and situations. That's the reason for the promise to persevere.

To promise to 'proclaim Christ' does not mean that we have to jump on soapboxes and harangue others. It does mean that there are moments in our lives when we can quietly and effectively let it be known that we are Christian, either by something we say or do.

The capacity to 'seek and serve Christ in all persons' is central to Christian faith. Because God took human form in Jesus, we think of a reflection of that divine nature as being in every human being we encounter. Our belief that God took human form in Jesus is the basis for not only this promise but the next and last one. It asks us to 'strive for justice and peace' and to 'respect the dignity of every human being.'

Striving for justice and peace may draw us beyond our private lives. It may involve us in the structures and institutions of society. When this happens, we are doing only what our Lord did from time to time. He knew very clearly that good and evil struggle, not only in our personal lives but also in public life, not only in individuals but also in our institutions.

The more we think about these promises, the more we realize that Christian faith is not a casual commitment!

I baptize you in the name of the Father, and of the Son, and of the Holy Spirit. I sign you with the sign of the cross.

When a child is carried to a font or an adult bends over the font, when in some parts of the world the action is carried out on the bank of a river or on the edge of a lake or sea, the flow of time stops. This action has remained the same over two millennia and is about to enter its third. Here we see the birth of a new Christian.

Two things are done. Water is poured and the sign of the cross is made. Certain words are said, which may at first seem strange. We hear a kind of formula. We are saying something about the God in whose presence we stand and to whom we offer this person's life. We are acknowledging God to be creator of all, to have come among us in Jesus Christ, and to dwell in our lives as *Spirit*. We now ask that this become the central belief and trust of the person being baptized. As Christians, we believe that to look at creation and all of human experience through this lens of faith is to make sense of human life.

After the water has been poured on the person, the sign of the cross is made on their forehead. It is an outward sign of what has just happened. We have offered this person to our Lord Jesus Christ. This person will now be identified with him for the rest of his or her life. He or she may not always think or act as if this were so, and may even at some stage repudiate this moment. But what is done in this moment can never be undone. This person is now part of Jesus Christ. Because the cross is the symbol of the central event of his life, his death and resurrection, it is marked on a Christian to say that, at this moment, this person has begun a new life.

The new Christian is now brought from the font and presented to the Christian community. A prayer is said. Notice how it speaks of a 'new life of grace.' Nowhere is the popular 1960s statement more true than at Christian baptism. It says, 'This is the first day of the rest of your life.'

So it is, and, as at any birthday celebration, certain gifts are offered. Even the words that describe these gifts are lovely. For the newly baptized, we ask four things—'an enquiring and discerning heart, courage to will and to persevere, a spirit to know and love God, and the gift of joy and wonder' in everything. Quite a birthday party!

Receive the light of Christ to show that you have passed from darkness to light.

An adult or child has just been baptized and presented to the worshipping community. One of the people around the font now takes a candle, goes to the tall Paschal or Easter candle, and touches the smaller candle to the flame. This smaller candle is now given to the newly baptized adult. It will also be given to the newly baptized child, if he or she is old enough to take it. If not, it will be given to someone in the family, or a Godparent, and the words above will be said.

Light is one of the most ancient and powerful symbols in Christian faith. Light symbolizes many things—the presence of God, guidance, hope, grace. At this moment, as the tiny flame is handed over, it has one clear meaning. This is the light of Christ being offered to the new Christian.

Jesus said that he had come to be light in the world. He offered himself to people as light for the journey through life. This is the sense in which Jesus is being offered at this moment. We are saying, 'There are times of darkness in every life. Take this light. There are times of feeling lost, times of wandering aimlessly. Take this light.' These are some of the words left unspoken as we hand over this light.

On another level, something else is being said. Just as the flame symbolizes something offered to us from *beyond* ourselves, so it also symbolizes something already *within* ourselves. In one of the four Gospels written about Jesus, the one written by John, we are told that there is a light that lightens everyone who comes into the world—the light of the Holy Spirit. In other words, if we can imagine God as light or flame, we are saying that a tongue of that flame burns in each one of us by virtue of our having been born. As with any flame, this flicker of God's Spirit within us needs to be cared for and nourished. Who better to do this than the people who have been involved in this person's baptism? For a child, the love of parents and Godparents can be a channel. For an adult, the love of a spouse or a dear friend can help achieve what God intends for this person.

Let us welcome the newly baptized.

It isn't just a coincidence that there is a congregation here. The fact that they are here expresses one of the key things about a baptism. Strictly speaking, the statement 'someone has been baptized' is incomplete. What should follow are the words 'into the Christian Church' or 'into the Christian faith' or 'into the Christian worshipping community.'

Why is this so important? Because Christian faith throws out a challenge to aspects of Western culture. Christian faith pushes at the assumption that we are complete as individuals. It does not for a moment deny that our individuality is of supreme importance. In fact, this becomes more and more important as we live in an increasingly technological culture. But Christian faith adds that we are most truly individuals when we live and function in community with others. An integral part of our individual selves is our ability to develop and enjoy relationships.

Obviously all those in the congregation cannot become intimately involved in the life of the person just baptized. None of us could handle it, if this happened to us! What is really being said as the people give the newly baptized this warm welcome? (By the way, in some congregations this moment of welcome includes a hearty round of hand-clapping.)

The people present at this baptism are saying they will accept responsibility for the continued life of this church, so that its gifts and resources will remain available to the person being baptized. They are saying they will see to it that this will continue to be a place where a child can grow happily in Christian faith, and where an adult can mature in faith for the rest of their life journey. They are saying God will be worshipped, the sacraments will be celebrated, the Word of God will be taught, prayer will be offered, and friendship will be available here. These people are offering this place and all other places of Christian community as places of love, joy, peace, faith, and hope—priceless realities that all of us will always need.

These are all reasons why the people of this community who are watching this baptism are far more than spectators.

At Confirmation, Reception, or Reaffirmation

Because life is a process of growing and changing, over time we find that we need to renew the commitments we have made. We may suddenly realize that a friendship is beginning to fade, and have to decide whether we are going to let this happen or do something about it. The same is true for a marriage relationship. That is why some couples renew their marriage vows at various intervals as the years go by.

The realization that a single Yes does not suffice forever is valid in the practice of our Christian faith. After all, this too is a relationship, a relationship with God through Jesus. If we were children at the time of our baptism, others said Yes for us. There comes a time when we need to say that Yes for ourselves. We need to *confirm* it. In the prayer on page 161 of *The Book of Alternative Services,* the bishop lays hands on us in the name of the Christian community and prays for us.

Sometimes, for any of a number of reasons, we may wish to move from one Christian tradition to another. This should never be done casually. We first need to be quite certain that we cannot and should not stay in the tradition we know and where we are known. But when we have made the decision to change, we then need to make every effort to become familiar with the tradition we have been drawn to—experiencing its worship, learning its story, becoming aware of how it has received the faith, how it is taught, what it expects of those who join its life. These and many other things should be known before we commit ourselves to the new community. When at last we do so, we will appreciate this prayer for our *reception*.

Again for any number of reasons, we may find that our faith has become weak and tired. We may have moved away from Christian faith and the community because of something that happened in our lives, and then resolved to return. We may recently have decided to take on some responsibility or particular piece of service in the church itself or in society. In any of these circumstances, we may wish to have this prayer of *reaffirmation* said for us.

It may very well be that on the day of baptism an individual or a number of individuals will offer themselves for one of these actions above. In each of these situations, the self-offering of the person is acknowledged and responded to with a particularly beautiful prayer:

> Almighty and everlasting God, let your fatherly hand ever be over these your servants; let your Holy Spirit ever be with them; and so lead them in the knowledge and obedience of your word, that they may serve you in this life, and dwell with you in the life to come; through Jesus Christ our Lord.

Notice the images used to show our relationship with God. We are shown God and the love of God sheltering us, constantly with us, leading us encouragingly, dwelling with us faithfully.

A final word. There are some things worth reaching for in life, things that can make all the difference. Christian faith and Christian community are among these. Those who possess them will tell you that they are the greatest things of all. May you discover them and find blessing in and through them.